ULTIMATE ISSUES

ALSO IN THE R. C. SPROUL LIBRARY

ULTIMATE ISSUES

R. C. SPROUL

PUBLISHING
P.O. BOX 817 • PHILLIPSBURG • NEW JERSEY 08865-0817

Page design and typesetting by Dog Eared Design, Sisters, Oregon, www.dogeareddesign.com

Printed in the United States of America

LIBRARY OF CONGRESS CATALOGING-IN-PUBLICATION DATA

Sproul, R. C. (Robert Charles), 1939–
    Ultimate Issues / R. C. Sproul.
        p. cm. — (R.C. Sproul library)
    Originally published: Grand Rapids, Mich. : Baker Books, ©1996.
    ISBN 0-87552-625-X
    1. Belief and doubt. 2. Faith. 3. Truth. I. Title.
    BD215.S68 2005
    230—dc22   2004057514

Contents

INTRODUCTION

Order the java.
Pull up some chairs.
Let's talk.

AMERICANS TODAY REALLY don't think too much about philosophy. Some philosophizing has been going on. But the quality of reflection and debate is fairly poor; and I hope it will not sink lower still. Where can we find a gathering of worthy thinkers on college campuses? Where are those whose intellectual swords are sharpened and ready for a duel? Ah, for the sound of clashing ideas, the passionate exchange of thoughts! In recent years I have had more trouble making people passionate about ideas. That never used to be a problem. What passes for intellectual ardor today is about as sharp as a pair of hedge clippers honed on politically-correctisms and then left outside overnight in the rain.

But wait! All is not lost! I think a better day has dawned, thanks at least in part to the popularity of the coffeehouse.

Coffeehouses have been around for thousands of years—long before coffee became an excuse for them. At least one coffeehouse is mentioned in chapter 17 of the New Testament's Book of Acts. The Christian leader Paul loved nothing more than a good battle of ideas. He happened to be in Athens, the world center of academia and culture, so he naturally found his way to a hillside amphitheater called the Areopagus. Here the learned gathered daily to wage verbal warfare for the sheer joy of hearing themselves think and talk. Acts 17:21 says: "All the Athenians and the foreigners who lived there spent their time doing nothing but talking about and listening to the latest ideas."

No coffee, but this was definitely a coffeehouse.

Students in the late 1950s to early 1970s experienced the golden days of coffeehouses. The best of them had a readily identifiable ambiance. The building was slightly dingy and located in a disreputable part of town, yet not too far from campus. Lighting was held to a bare minimum (votive candles), mostly to illuminate folksingers in jeans who provided not-ready-for-prime-time background music. Round tables were spread with red-checkered, crumb-littered plastic tablecloths. These tables were never quite large enough to accommodate chairs for a good discussion, so some people sat on the floor. They compared existentialist philosophers and the Platonic idealism of Andy Warhol's latest Campbell's Soup can. In this Areopagus, confidence and desire counted, plus an adequate command of a large vocabulary. The important thing was to sound deep; actually knowing something about the subject at hand was optional.

I'm happy for the coffeehouse comeback. Now maybe we can get back to addressing the lasting issues of philosophy.

What are these lasting or "ultimate" issues? In the ancient Areopagus, Paul said the ultimate issue was the search for an eternal source of truth. He had especially noticed one altar among the statues of gods and goddesses in the Athenian pantheon. The altar to which he referred can be seen by tourists in the city of Athens today, for it stood strong and solid, without any statuary to break and crumble away. On that altar the Greek inscription can be translated: "TO AN UNKNOWN GOD."

Among the ideas and ideals of our time, a great temple has been erected to take the place of that altar in Athens. The ancient Athenian inscription was somewhat hopeful. Its builders assumed that an unknown God existed and might be known. Today's altar is etched with a darker dedication:

"TO AN UNKNOWABLE GOD."

Or worse:

"TO A NONEXISTENT, USELESS, AND IRRELEVANT GOD."

A folksinger in the Areopagus would have dropped her guitar when Paul said: "Let me tell you all about your unknown God." What happened next is really interesting. Everyone was all ears as Paul began describing a God who had created nature and humankind, a God about whom the Greek poets had sung unawares.

Paul put a name to that God, *Jesus,* who had become a man, had died, and then had conquered death by divine power and justice. Suddenly the philosophers saw where this was headed. Only a few wanted to hear more.

Why do you suppose interest and intellectual openness so quickly vanished? That still happens in coffeehouse discussions, and for the same reason: *Ultimate answers to ultimate issues are extremely uncomfortable.*

But even if you do feel a little uptight, let's gather in the coffeehouse to speak of ultimate things. The light is low, the comradeship cozy. The music is slow and a little mournful. Your view of reality is warmed and ready to serve over espresso.

I'm betting a discussion of ultimate issues may answer some important questions.

ONE

WHEN WORLDS COLLIDE

"Well, I think people are just as valuable as animals. I think it is a combined thing. We are all alive. We are all living creatures. We all deserve the same."

"I don't think people are any more important than animals. Every living thing has a right to be heard, and we are not to say whether we are more important than just a dog or cat."

"I don't think we should just go on as if there is no god. I think we should go on as if there was a god."

"People are more important than animals. Mainly just because animals can't speak for themselves."

"I think that if there wasn't a god everything would be permissible because there would be no guidelines for us, because he didn't set the guidelines for us to start off with."

"You can have a sense of right and wrong without being necessarily Christian or Buddhist or Islamic."

"The value of individuals and people has to do with being able to take care of what is around you, being able to take care of animals and plants and your environment and each other, which humans can uniquely do."

IN THE SUMMER OF 1994 astronomers were treated to an unprecedented spectacle. Through the modern technology of the Hubble space telescope, mounted on a satellite outside the earth's atmosphere, they received telescopic photographs of a massive collision between our largest planet neighbor, Jupiter, and fragments from a gigantic comet that had broken apart and spread its pieces throughout the solar system.

The event started a debate in the scientific community. Jupiter is a lot larger target for space waste to hit than the earth. But if it could happen to Jupiter, couldn't it happen to this planet? If even one chunk of comet made a bank shot off Europe, the neighborhood could become a pretty unpleasant place. One astronomer advised us to relax—the odds of getting in the way of a space bullet are only once every million years or so. Carl Sagan was more concerned. He said the odds against such a collision happening in the next hundred years are only a thousand to one. That still doesn't seem too likely, but considering the results of a collision, he isn't at all happy with those odds.

Whereas worlds don't collide every day, worldviews do.

A worldview is simply *a view of the world,* a way of looking at life. It is the framework we use to make sense of things. Each of us has our own perspective. It doesn't precisely match anyone else's. So let's throw onto the table a proposition that may seem to be absurd: There are two worldviews and only two. These two views of reality take on individual hues and shapes, but every human being old enough to form conclusions about the surrounding environment will adopt one of the two fundamental positions.

These two worldviews bump into one another all the time. And, yes, the collision is loud and stirs up a lot of dust.

A System Designed by Smorgasbord

Think how hard it is to go even one day without having a disagreement with another person. Some interpersonal problems arise simply because I want my way instead of yours. Other conflicts happen when two people simply have a different view of life.

Both sides may wonder, "Why can't we agree on this? We agree on so many things, but when we get into this area, then look out." Things become explosive when incompatible philosophies enter into a conversation. Sometimes the arguments that seem to result from stubborn refusals to see the other person's perspective are really worldview collisions. When we blow away all the smoke and pull away all the camouflage our minds have erected, it is hard—even impossible—to find something we think or do that isn't influenced by our worldview and the particular system of philosophy we have built on our worldview foundation.

Now in one sense, a worldview *is* a system. Systems should, by definition, be systematic—integrated, consistent, and coherent. Unfortunately, not one of us has a perfectly consistent, coherent system for interpreting life. That isn't surprising. We add to our worldview information gained from wide variety of sources, from parents to kindergarten teachers, from college professors to television, and from novels to the mechanic who tunes the car. A lot of information comes into the mind's central receiving station. Most of it travels on through undisturbed, but we latch onto a bit of it here and there that sounds interesting. These odds and ends are filtered through experience. These are ideas we test in the laboratory of life, only it is not a very scientific experiment. Those pieces that we decide to keep are welded, somewhat haphazardly, onto our system for thinking and our values base for living. That cobbled conglomeration may not look like much, but it is all ours and we are quite fond of it. We would hate to trade it in, even for something better.

Another way of describing the process is to think of our life philosophy as a four-course dinner that has been assembled at a smorgasbord food bar. We choose a little soup here, a little salad over there, and some entree over here. Vegetables and dessert get all mixed together. Nothing looks quite like it did in the serving dishes. The inevitable result of our do-it-your-self system building is conflict. We walk through life cherishing mutually exclusive ideas, ideas that simply do not logically work together. We have to make allowances and logical leaps to tie it all together, and the result never really satisfies. If views of reality butt against one another within my own head, imagine what happens when my illogical view of life comes in contact with your illogical view of life. Sometimes the result is about the same as when Jupiter met the comet—a pothole extraordinaire.

Between Two Poles

Now look at the big picture, the biggest system that can be made from all the little, mixed-up pieces. Each of our inconsequential ideas relates in some way to a philosophy. That system is the product of an even more ultimate core view. All sorts of differing philosophies compete with each other. Marxism debates existentialism debates logical positivism debates various humanisms. But these thought-systems can collide without essentially changing the individual. They are small asteroids, or middle-level thought managers. All these systems can be divided between two giant worlds, which are in inevitable conflict with one another. All the small philosophical moons revolve around one of two worlds: *theism* or *atheism.* Theism maintains that a god of some sort is the ultimate cause and sustainer of all that is. Atheism, meaning a-theism or non-theism, rejects the concept of a god in any meaningful form.

If we were to illustrate the relationship between these two systems on a chalkboard, it would be difficult to find one large enough to do justice to the magnitude of their difference. Let us say that in our coffeehouse I have installed a blackboard that extends from one side of the building to the other. On one side of this blackboard I write the word *theism.* Then I walk all the way across the room, and on the far side I chalk in the word *atheism.* The length of empty board separating the two concepts would begin to dramatize the enormous gulf that separates these "ultimate" perspectives.

That image of the huge chalkboard illustrates another point about the worldviews. We have said that no two people have precisely the same view of life. How do two uncompromising antitheses allow such diversity? We can rephrase the question in the analogy of the comet striking Jupiter. If the worldviews are so distant from one another, why do they keep colliding so viciously?

The reason is that none of us lives fully at one end or the other. Each of us tries to live somewhere between the two poles. We are most comfortable with a dialectic worldview. Deep inside we know that these two propositions are incompatible. Deep inside, though, we don't particularly want to admit that Supreme Being calls the shots. If there is a Creator God as is posited by the Bible, we are accountable to that Being. We lose freedom. We lose the confident feeling that I am the most important thing in the universe. That creates tension.

But then intellectual honesty reminds us that if no one is in charge, we are in a supersonic jet with no pilot. We can't even guarantee that the natural laws will continue to function in a safe and rational manner. The atheist must assume that a whole lot of nothing, or some eternally existing gases, came together in a totally random fashion and made themselves into all that is. In that scenario there can be no "laws" that hold things together. A law means there is intelligence to the design and it governs the law. Not only does that view seem unreasonable; it strikes me with all the discomfort Carl Sagan finds in the possibility of a comet–earth accident. Beyond that, humans seem to feel an existential need to look to something bigger than themselves. To be the ultimate thing in the universe is to feel the separation from all other things in the universe. I don't honestly think that anyone is really wired to enjoy being a god. At least there seems little evidence that the convinced atheist is a happy or self-actualized believer.

Life in the Either-Or

No one is a perfectly consistent theist. No one is a perfectly consistent atheist. We borrow some ideas from theism, we borrow some ideas from atheism, and then we try to somehow make them work together. Thesis meets antithesis, and the outcome is synthesis—a mediating new thesis that is somewhere in-between. The dialectic approach has so pervaded our thought processes that this seems to be a workable sort of compromise. It is not, for a reason that can be expressed in science fiction terms. The crew of the USS *Voyager* comes across a technique for mining a glob of antimatter. This is an exciting breakthrough, for at last they are able to mix pure *matter* with pure *antimatter* to make a third substance called *sort-a-matter*. But matter and antimatter do not easily coexist. Try to put them together, and the whole television series blows to smithereens.

Can we have a god-no-god-sort-a-god dialectical universe? No synthesis can exist between mutually exclusive truth statements.

The foundation to all our thinking is really an either-or perspective. The Danish philosopher Søren Kierkegaard once wrote a little book with that title, *Either-Or*. As a philosopher, Kierkegaard was aware that there is such a fallacy or logical error in thinking called the "either-or fallacy." This error in thought occurs when people demand a choice between two options when there are actually three, four, or a whole lot more possible choices. Such a choice is not, then, either-or.

Kierkegaard, however, was not stating a logical fallacy as he considered the cases for and against the existence of God. Either God exists or he doesn't exist; there is no third alternative. Kierkegaard set that issue squarely before us, because he knew that each person's answer to that either-or question establishes a system of conviction that influences thoughts on every other question. He restated the "either-or" proposition so that it was no longer a fallacy. If I have many options from which to choose and I make my decision, that act of choice somehow relates to how I perceive life with or without the existence of God. On one level my decision cannot be stated in either-or terms, but most fundamentally my decision is made because of my either-or stand between theism and antheism.

Let's imagine for a moment that after establishing the conviction that a Creator-Ruler God really exists, you are awakened by the red-orange glow of a sunrise shining through the window. Contemplating the view from bed, you are struck by the beauty of the design of a sunrise.

The alternative: "Lot of dust floating around out here today."

Should you get up? The tasks awaiting you at work don't promise much excitement. But that's all right. Even dull days are gifts that can be enjoyed.

The alternatives: (1) Another day, another dollar to keep the wolf from the door. (2) Wonder how many sick days I have left? I think I'll take one and just sleep in.

The morning paper tells abut a comet colliding with Jupiter. Oh, well, thank heaven things are under control!

The alternative: There's always something new to worry about. What's the point of things when we may go up like a cosmic fire cracker next week?

In the car heading for work your mind drifts to Karen and Sabrina. Both are fun to be with and attractive, and you've been thinking a lot about seriously dating one of them. Karen promises excitement. She hints she might be willing to move in with you. You wouldn't even think of asking Sabrina to do something like that. But you both have a faith that is enjoyable to share on a deeper level. It does seem to help her be more confident when she faces problems.

The alternative? You can work through that one on your own.

Along the way you pass a motorist having car trouble. You have a few minutes to give him a lift and you are inclined to stop. Why? It just seems natural to help someone else.

The alternative: "I'll stop if I feel like it. Helping somebody makes me feel worthwhile. And isn't that the only thing that really separates us from other animals?

Those sorts of thoughts and decisions are rattling through your head and it isn't even 8 in the morning. Not every choice is conscious or involves ethical issues. Either the theist or the atheist may stop to help the motorist and make similar choices on a lot of other decisions. But when that happens these identical decisions come from very different motivations. The atheist can enjoy the colorful sunrise, but not as a created, designed thing. The theist may worry over what is in the news, but a consistent theist works from the assumption that what is reported is not a random act of blind chance.

The Ultimate Good at the Center

The theist thinks *theocentrically;* the reality of God moves toward the center of all that is evaluated and analyzed. *God* is an idea with enormous implications.

If I am convinced that God does not exist or that anything "up there" must be irrelevant, that denial becomes the very foundation of my thinking about life, death, and what has value. In fact,

I will tend to think *anthropocentrically,* that is, from a human-centered perspective. It is no accident that the person-centered mind-set we call "modern humanism" always fits under the category of atheism. Since there is no god, then the highest being in the known cosmos of our experience is the human animal.

From that viewpoint, a human can only be a cosmic accident, a grown-up germ who has fortuitously emerged from the slime. Human origin is from nothingness and human destiny is toward nothingness—yet the humanist leads the parade crusading for human rights, human values, and human dignity.

Wait a minute! If I am a cosmic accident, if I begin in insignificance and I end in insignificance, how can I possibly have significance in-between? The humanist answers that humanity gives us a sort of charm. We are biased because we are people. We like to think we are important and valuable. That idea cannot come from an atheistic system because the atheistic system undermines any possibility of human significance or importance. In the last century's most well-known atheistic system, communism, human importance derives from the state. People have significance only as they relate to a collective whole. The individual is not a major concern.

In the humanist system, the good of the species is all-important. You may have run across a favorite philosophy or ethics class scenario. In this scenario an atomic war has broken out and a group of people have minutes to blast off in a spaceship before the earth becomes uninhabitable. A dozen people stand at the launching pad, but the ship has only enough oxygen, food, and water aboard for six. Who will be sent off to live and who will wave good-bye and then die? Obviously the decision will involve picking individuals who can reproduce and sustain a new generation of humans. Individually these people are unimportant. They live or die through their contribution to the collective species.

Such a view places a person on a common level with the beasts. We are just more sophisticated animals.

A Student's-Eye View

At Ligonier Ministries we decided to conduct a kind of worldview survey. So we took cameras and tape recorders to high school and college campuses around North America. We asked some randomly selected students what they think about the relative value and importance of human beings as compared to animals. Let's see how they responded:

> *"I don't know if humans are more important than animals. Part of the reason I am in college is to figure out these types of things."*

> *"Well, I think people are just as valuable as animals. I think it is a combined thing. We are all alive. We are all living creatures. We all deserve the same."*

> *"By far people are way more important than animals. I mean, I consider myself to be a little bit right-wing, conservative, and all these save-the-animals people, well, personally they annoy me."*

> *"I don't think people are any more important than animals. Every living thing has a right to be heard, and we*

are not to say whether we are more important than just a dog or cat."

"People are more important than animals. Mainly just because animals can't speak for themselves."

"The value of individuals and people has to do with being able to take care of what is around you, being able to take care of animals and plants and your environment and each other, which humans can uniquely do."

"Human life is important. It is sacred. The Bible said we were set apart from the animals. We have a higher position."

"When people kill animals to eat, I kind of cringe a little bit. You know, that personally is my opinion. I thought we abolished slavery."

Obviously, these students express different opinions. The first person was somewhat agnostic about the question and said, "I'm not sure. One reason I am going to college is to inquire and to investigate such questions." Others spoke assertively. One person who said people are more important explained that he is "right-wing," though a high value judgment for humanity is not unique to a political view. Most people said that, fundamentally, there is no difference—we are the same as other animals because we are all alive.

The latter comment is most intriguing. The way we exploit animals is wrong because slavery has ended. Notice the value judgment in this statement: "There is something inherently wrong with slavery. We are opposed to slavery as an evil. What difference does it make, ultimately, whether we put a horse in a harness and attach him to the buggy and beat him on the back with a whip to transport us around, or if we hitch up people and beat them on the back? After all, we are all the same."

The dream of the American Civil Rights Movement was persuasively stated by Martin Luther King Jr. King protested vigorously against discrimination. The heroic woman Rosa Parks ignited a nation when she refused to sit in the back of the bus because of the color of her skin. But if we are all germs, who cares who sits in the back of the bus? What difference does it make whether one person enslaves another, human or animal? We make value judgments about the worth and the value of human dignity on the basis of a philosophical foundation. And if that foundation says from the outset that human life is insignificant because we are destined to return to the slime from which we came, why should we care?

The Content of Nothingness

Now, plug these thoughts into that middle ground between theism and atheism. Theists borrow ideas from atheists. Those who identify themselves as Christians embrace ideas fundamentally opposed to belief in God without realizing the contradiction. This is not a new problem. The Old Testament tells the history of the nation of Israel. Israel was set apart by God to be a holy nation. But in the end they failed to act like a set-apart people, so the nation failed. The reason was that they indiscriminately blended values and concepts from opposing systems.

The Jewish people worshiped God on the Sabbath, but the rest of the week they wanted to amuse themselves on the playground of the false gods. They devoted part of their religion to the God of the universe, Yahweh, but then they also built shrines and temples and statues and idols to pagan gods. God rebuked his people for trying to live in two worlds at the same time.

This conflict may be seen most clearly in ethics. If God does not exist, our ethical systems are arbitrary. Friedrich Nietzsche said that since God is dead we must embrace nihilism, a recognition of what he calls *das Nichtige*—the nothingness. Later, Jean-Paul Sartre called human life a useless passion. Sarte meant that the human has strong feelings, which is what passion is about. We care deeply about things. But Sartre said it is useless, futile passion. With no ultimate truth, there is no standard of value, no norm of right and wrong. We are left to flounder as we determine our own ethics.

We asked students how their affirmation or denial of the existence of God conditions their thinking about ethical behavior:

> *"I am the only human being that exists. Nobody else exists. Everything else is set up for my own personal enjoyment. Therefore, everything goes along to my own personal standards. So I have essentially become my own god. I mean, if he doesn't exist, then I am just going to take over the role."*

> *"I don't think we should just go on as if there is no god. I think we should go on as if there was a god."*

"I think that if there wasn't a god everything would be permissible because there would be no guidelines for us, because he didn't set the guidelines for us to start off with."

"You can have a sense of right and wrong without being necessarily Christian or Buddhist or Islamic."

"I would say people that don't believe in God practically get this sense of right and wrong from just courtroom situations, the way society views certain things. If society says that to kill someone is wrong, maybe they will feel that way because society says so. But they don't really have a religious basis for what they're feeling."

"People who do not believe in God as the origin of values and meanings in their life decide for themselves what is right and wrong. I know several people, in fact, my boyfriend, who do not believe in God. I think they basically believe in themselves."

"That's exactly why I think our country is in the state it is now. People don't have any governing body like that. So many people don't believe there is a higher being up there, so they just do what they want and that's why we have all these radicals. And people are saying I can choose this and I can choose that, and that's why there is no real standard of anything anymore, the way I see it."

Again we see the conflict. If there is no God, it comes down to personal choice. Ethics becomes a matter of personal preference. That works for those willing to live superficially. Inevitably in critical thought the implications of a godless universe without ultimate norms lead to a philosophy of despair. The issues boil down to full-orbed theism or an atheism cut off from all hope. All the props are knocked out from under us. We are left with Fyodor Dostoevsky's remark that if there is no god, all things are permissible.

Murder? Rape? Extortion? All are permitted. There is no such thing as evil.

Think about that seriously and the only possible response is despair.

Nevermore

What is a coffeehouse without poetry? Edgar Allan Poe anguished over the question of ultimate issues. His most famous poem, "The Raven," penetrates the deepest feelings of the human heart before this issue:

> *Once upon a midnight dreary, while I pondered, weak*
> *   and weary,*
> *Over many a quaint and curious volume of forgotten lore—*
> *While I nodded, nearly napping, suddenly there came a tapping,*
> *As of someone gently rapping, rapping at my chamber door.*
> *" 'Tis some visitor," I muttered, "tapping at my chamber door—*
> *Only this and nothing more."*
>
> *Ah, distinctly I remember it was in the bleak December:*
> *And each separate dying ember wrought its ghost upon the floor.*

Here is a man who has lost the woman he loves. Death has intruded and taken from him the person in whom he invested his love, his hope, his entire humanity. His melancholy reverie as he ponders these things is interrupted by a rude visitor from the animal kingdom. An ominous bird flies in and perches above the door. The hero starts conversing with this bird. But the damnable bird has a one-word vocabulary. Every time the writer seeks hope and looks for answers, the same reply comes: "Nevermore."

At the end of the poem comes a rising crescendo of despair, and in his frustration, the man cries out to this bird,

> *"Prophet," said I, "thing of evil!—prophet still, if bird or devil!—*
> *Whether Tempter sent, or whether tempest tossed thee here ashore,*
> *Desolate, yet all undaunted, on this desert land enchanted—*
> *On this home by horror haunted—tell me truly, I implore—*
> *Is there—is there balm in Gilead?—tell me—tell me, I implore!"*
> *Quoth the Raven, "Nevermore."*

"Is there balm in Gilead" The question is a question of hope. Is there any hope for the destiny of my beloved? The bird's reply remains the same, "No, there is not." Finally, the man says,

> *"Be that word our sign of parting, bird or fiend!" I shrieked, upstarting—*
> *"Get thee back into the tempest and the night's Plutonian shore!*
> *Leave no black plume as a token of that lie thy soul hath spoken!*
> *Leave my loneliness unbroken—quit the bust above my door!*
> *Take thy beak from out my heart, and take thy form from off my door!"*

Quoth the Raven, "Nevermore."
And the Raven, never flitting, still is sitting, still is sitting
On the pallid bust of Pallas just above my chamber door;
and his eyes have all the seeming of a demon's that is dreaming.
And the lamplight o'er him streaming throws his shadow on
*   the floor;*
And my soul from out that shadow that lies floating on the floor
Shall be lifted—nevermore!

Poe understood the antithesis. He understood the questions and he didn't try to play games. He was no syncretist. If no one is home, there is no hope—not now nor evermore.

QUESTIONS FOR STUDY AND DISCUSSION

1. What makes the propositions of theism and atheism incompatible?
2. In what specific ways does your worldview affect the way you live and think?
3. Why does atheism inevitably lead to the conclusion that humans are insignificant?
4. Why do humans have more value than animals?
5. What effect does the acceptance of the existence of God have on one's ethical system?
6. Why does an atheistic worldview lead to despair?

THE GOD WHO IS THERE

"I think God created the universe, but there is still that little doubt in my mind that it could be the Big Bang theory. I mean, I haven't really researched that."

"I think the universe came from God. He said 'Let there be light,' and there was light and the earth and everything like that."

"I don't believe in the Big Bang theory or evolution in the sense that we came from amoebas and down that whole line."

"I believe in the scientific element of it, the Big Bang and everything like that. But sometimes when I just see flowers or I see like a little baby, or some things that I just don't know how they would have gotten there unless there had been a God."

"Well, I believe it was a combination of God and science. I think that he made the science half of it. He made the Big Bang. I think he made that happen."

"Everyone says 'God created it.' Great! Where did he get what he used to create it from?"

DEFINING MOMENTS OF CRISIS punctuate every nation's history. By the time these crises are resolved, a new direction has been established for the following generations. The American Revolution was such a watershed. The American attitude of "Manifest Destiny" and the American experiment with democracy were born in the struggle. Both dramatically shaped the North American continental and world history.

But if we look beyond parochial interests to the whole of human history, we must take note of another revolution that was occurring in Europe even as the colonial militia gathered on Lexington green. This watershed crossed borders and continents. It washed over the entire Western world and sent ripples across the rest of humanity. It was a revolution of the mind far more radical than any political movement. It was the *Kantian revolution.* The Kantian revolution is the greatest worldview collision point in Western cultural history. Worldviews collided because Immanuel Kant separated reason from the knowledge of God.

Sitting around the table at our coffeehouse, we must leave an empty chair, for it will be filled by the shadow of Immanuel Kant. Even those who have never sat through a class in philosophy are intellectual godchildren of this great thinker and his idea revolution, which began with publication of Kant's monumental book, *The Critique of Pure Reason.*

Kant was a strange revolutionary. In the years between his birth in 1724 and his death in 1804, he never traveled farther than one hundred miles from his birthplace. He was a man of such meticulous, boring predictability that neighbors could reliably set their clocks by his daily constitutional walk. This inconspicuous philosopher's one truly influential book fell like a bombshell. Kant did not make the case for atheism. Rather, he made rational agnosticism possible. Kant's critique rejected three historical arguments for the existence of God that had stood since the founding of medieval universities. These decisive arguments established (or so people believed) the existence of a self-existent Author of the universe.

The *ontological argument* assumed a definition of God: The Creator must be a perfect Being. Anselm of Canterbury argued that even people who don't believe in a God would define the God they don't believe in as infinite and perfect. Can a flawless Being exist in thought but not in reality? No, answered Anselm, for a nonexistent perfect God would be flawed by nonexistence. If such a Being can be conceived of, that Being must exist. Therefore, to conceive of a God is to prove a priori that there is a God.

The *cosmological argument* is not quite so obtuse. It dates back to the Greek philosophers and remains in use today. This argument has a few variations. The Greeks reasoned that for every movement there is something that sets the movement in motion. Movement requires a mover. But that means that at the very beginning something had to be moved by an Un-moved Mover. Someone had to start that first ball rolling. A popular form of the cosmological argument starts from a simple premise: "Stuff exists." How did the stuff we see come into existence? Something obviously comes from something, so where did the first something come from? There had to be a First cause of what is, and whatever or whoever that First Cause is, there we will find God.

The *teleological argument* is even older and simpler. This is an argument from design. It says: "Look around at the world. You not only see stuff; you see well-made stuff." Some thought obviously went into the chemical composition of the stars. The intricacy of the flower and the way the human body works shout that God exists and that God is quite a Designer. One of the most beautiful statements of the theological argument comes in the poetry of the Bible's Psalm 19. It begins:

> The heavens declare the glory of God;
>> the skies proclaim the work of his hands.
> Day after day they pour forth speech;
>> night after night they display knowledge.
> There is no speech or language
>> where their voice is not heard.
> Their voice goes out into all the earth,
>> their words to the ends of the world.

Silencing the Voices

Kant was the first to successfully take on the big-three arguments for God's existence. He did so by attacking causal thought. Causal thinking governs much scientific inquiry. If you are sick, doctors look for a cause. In physics if there is a phenomenon of light, we look for its source. When that comet hit Jupiter, we stared at it to see the effects. In Kant's lifetime, as today, scientists in every discipline were committed to this approach to problem solving. They reasoned backward from effects to causes.

But Kant asserted that our ability to answer ultimate questions in this way is severely limited. We are locked into a world in which we are dependent on what our senses tell us. Sensual data may be adequate for causal thinking in biology, physics, and medicine, but we can't use that approach to cross into the realm of metaphysics. We can't deduce a Creator from the creation.

Since humans are quite adept at imagining what does not exist, Kant said, the ontological argument is no true proof for the existence of God. The cosmological and telelolgical arguments only state the ontological argument in a different way. Therefore, we can't reason our way back to God. Neither can we derive ethical standards from the will of God. Modern philosophy thus was born.

What a revolutionary thought! The strongest intellectual argument for theism in all history was crippled. This opened the door for modernity and secularism, the effects of which we're just now starting to understand.

If He Is There, He Is Angry

With that history in mind, we return to atheism and theism, the two competing paradigms. Agnosticism is a subspecies of atheism. The agnostic may be less militant than the atheist, but the agnostic equally refuses to affirm the existence of God. So at the point where agnostic and theistic worldviews meet, opposites collide.

Certainly the reflections of Kant collide with the thinking of Paul in the Bible. Kant said we cannot assume the eternal God from nature. Paul counters in his letter to Christians in Rome that we can know a great deal about God by looking at creation; the problem is that we don't *want to know* the God revealed in creation.

Kant and Paul think contradictory thoughts because of their epistemologies. As father of the Enlightenment, Kant assumed the universe to be a *closed system.* Nothing and no one was working from the outside in. This being the case, we are on our own when it comes to discerning reality. We collect data for evaluating the difference between truth and falsehood only by means of our senses. And senses are easily fooled by the appearance of reality.

The theist Paul assumed that the system is open. God transcends both the system and our ability to evaluate. We can see evidence for God in nature from our fallible senses in scientific discovery. But ultimately we don't depend on those sensory data for knowledge. God desires that we know truth. He sets truth in every human heart.

But isn't Kant correct? If truth is so obviously at our disposal, why do we have antagonistic visions of truth warring against one another?

"Ah," Paul says, "that is the important question. We don't see the evidence, not because our senses are fooled, but because our mind is evil."

Paul says (in Romans 1:18) that the wrath of God is being revealed from heaven against wicked people who suppress the truth about him. God is disclosing anger. The Greek word used for anger is orge. This word stands behind the English word *orgy.* We think of an orgy as an unbridled, sexual, sensuous, bacchanalia. This sexual connotation of orgy contains the idea of passion. Passion in the realm of anger is what Paul has in mind. God is not mildly irritated or slightly annoyed, but is passionately furious. He is not simply angry at an impersonal thing called "evil." His anger is focused on the crime that evil commits against his character. The apostle is not declaring God's fury against hard-headed, militant atheists. God is angry at people universally. We have all personally committed the most primordial, elementary, and foundational act of defiance against God.

The crime is that we *suppress* or *repress* the truth. The Greek word used means that we incarcerate, hinder, or stifle truth. This is a cover-up, not of political scandal or embarrassing personal sin, but of truth about the nature, reality, and character of God. Paul explains in Romans 1:19–20 that "what may be known about God is plain to them, because God has made it plain to them. For since the creation of the world God's invisible qualities—his eternal power and divine nature—have been clearly seen, being understood from what has been made, so that men are without excuse."

God has made himself known through what he created. God himself is invisible; I cannot test and then attest my empirical perceptions of the Deity. But Paul argues that I can test and attest the nature of the world. Paul here uses the cosmological argument. He says that through science or simply through our wanderings around the created world, we can know that God exists and what he is like.

Kant says you can't move from perception of this world to perception of God. Paul replies that you can, for God has plainly shown himself through this world. You can't look at this world and miss God's signposts. Obviously Kant and Paul are on a collision course. Their conclusions about the possibility of knowing ultimate truth are mutually exclusive.

Paul goes on to say more. Not only can you find God through the evidence of his nature in creation, but you don't have to be a rocket scientist to discern the clues. The existence of God is so plain that everybody can get the message.

What excuse do you think people will use to explain their refusal to adore the living God? "Oh, God, if you only had given a clear revelation of yourself, I would have been your humble and devoted servant. But how could I know? I tried. I looked. I searched. But I couldn't find you."

That argument won't work when the physicist stands before God; it won't work even for the person who never attended a single biology lecture.

A God with a Bang

One of today's most persistent questions is the origin of the universe. I am personally intrigued by "Big Bang" cosmology. I find it agrees with several points of the biblical view of creation, though not all. But there are those who take speculation about origins a step further to say that the universe came into being by itself, accidentally, or perhaps it was already there from all eternity. Either explanation takes a lot more faith than to postulate that God created it all. In Romans 1 Paul regards it as intellectual dishonesty. The common purpose of wicked people is to come up with some explanation, any explanation, to avoid the assertion of a Creator.

On college campuses we asked students where they thought the universe came from. Here are some of their insights.

"Where did the world come from? Now that is a really difficult one because at school, even though I went to a Catholic school where we were taught that it was created by God. Then in science they also told us about the Big Bang theory. So I really don't know. I don't really have a standpoint on where the world came from. It was just there."

"I think the universe came from God. He said 'Let there be light,' and there was light and the earth and everything like that."

"I am about as atheistic as they come. I was baptized Catholic and brought up Episcopalian, but I don't really believe in any of that. I think I tend to favor the Big Bang theory."

"I don't believe in the Big Bang theory or evolution in the sense that we came from amoebas and down that whole line."

"I was raised in the Catholic tradition, so of course I was always taught to believe that God created everything. Then when I came to the reality of what's going on, I realized that that can't possibly be true. Maybe it is true in a metaphysical sense."

"Oh, yeah. God definitely created the world. No doubt. I'm not sure how he created it."

"Everyone says, 'God created it.' Great! Where did he get what he used to create it from?"

"Well, I believe it was a combination of God and science. I think that he made the science half of it. He made the Big Bang. I think he made that happen."

"I think God created the universe, but there is still that little doubt in my mind that it could be the Big Bang theory. I mean, I haven't really researched that."

"I believe in the scientific element of it, the Big Bang and everything like that. But sometimes when I just see flowers or I see like a little baby, or some things that I just don't know how they would have gotten there unless there had been a God."

"I have no idea where anything came from. I think about it, but I don't think I will ever find the answer. So to put too much thought into it would really kind of waste my time."

The most distressing response is the latter one, that the investigation of this ultimate question is really not worth the investment of time. Nothing is more important than to understand the dignity of existence. That is what is at stake in this question.

Notice how many students said they are impressed by the evidence for Big Bang cosmology. Yet some of them admit that they can't get past the idea that something must stand above even the Big Bang. Think about it. The theory suggests that all matter now existing in this incalculably large universe was, at one point some 15 or 18 billion years ago, all compressed into one infinitesimal point of singularity. That singularity presumably stayed in balance in an organized state of equilibrium. Then one Tuesday afternoon the law of inertia slipped and, bang!, it broke. I am willing to grant that a massive cosmic explosion may have distributed elements throughout the universe. But if we believe in the law of inertia, that things at rest tend to remain at rest unless acted upon by an outside cause, then we have every reason to assume that an outside cause struck the match or pushed the button or blinked.

No human reporter was on the scene to record the first event. We can extrapolate all the data we want, but the answer to the ultimate question will not be discovered using the scientific method. The ultimate question is not *what* happened. The ultimate question is what *caused* it to happen.

That ultimate question quickly becomes an ultimate, personal issue if the First Cause started the ball rolling and then guided subsequent actions. At the same time Kant lived, a group of lesser thinkers decided that they could grant a divine First Cause, without getting a personal god in the bargain. The theology of deism was very popular at the time of the American Revolution. Deism took into account that the natural sciences seemed to demand a Creator. Some sort of being swung the pendulum. But the deists' God was a child who gets out toys and then loses interest. God is not involved with creation at this moment and surely does not care about my puny little life in the gigantic scheme of things.

But this reasoning had a fatal flaw. If we concede a God who created the intricacy and complexity science reveals, then the idea of an unconcerned, uninvolved Maker is ludicrous. If atoms can be kept from drifting toward chaos, then the Mind at work is quite able to take note of human beings. Atheism/agnosticism is better. It might be hard to swallow, but the only rational alternative is a God who causes the effects. That puts me face to face with a personal, ultimate God who does care very much.

The Great Robbery

This issue is not unimportant. In the Bible, Paul writes that every human who contemplates the created world knows what kind of God is there. The tragedy is that people prefer to live in denial. They refuse to admit to a knowledge of God because they do not want to admit their dependence on God:

> For although they knew God, they neither glorified him as God nor gave thanks to him, but their thinking became futile and their foolish hearts were darkened. . . . They exchanged the truth of God for a lie and worshiped and served created things rather than the Creator— who is forever praised.
>
> (ROMANS 1:21, 25)

This is a stunning indictment. Paul is not talking about atheism. He describes a human religion that robs the God who is. Here is the scene Paul describes: I walk into an exhibition of European masterpieces, look around a bit, select a Peter Paul Rubens portrait, and remove it from the wall. Immediately, alarm sirens scream and thirty-two guards level guns at my head. But I refuse to let any of that bother me.

"What do you think you are doing?" the curator asks.

"This slab was hanging there. It's kind of colorful, and I thought it might make a nice welcome mat outside my back door."

"But this is worth millions of dollars. You may come to this museum to enjoy it. But what makes you think you can just take it away?"

"I do not believe that this is any more than a piece of flotsam that happens to have a pleasing shape and colors. It almost looks like somebody could have made it, but I refuse to accept any such fiction. I even refuse to accept that all that horrendous noise made a few moments ago has any connection with the fact that I pulled this thing off that wall, where it had no particular reason to be anyway."

Rubens has been dead many years and is not personally injured if I refuse to acknowledge his creation of a painting. People today who own his paintings have more at stake. I also have some stake in the matter. I live in the same reality in which Rubens created wonderful works and enriched the art world with his innovative techniques.

I would far rather rob Rubens of glory due him, than rob a living God of his rightful majesty, of his transcendent power, of his deity. Paul is saying that we know quite well that a Creator Deity exists, yet the universal human reaction is refusal to honor God or to be grateful. Refusal to acknowledge what you know to be true is the primary sin of the heart.

> You know that you are not God.
> You know that you are a creature.
> You know that you are finite, derived, and dependent.
> You know that you are morally responsible for your behavior.

At a specific moment in history you will stand before your Creator to give an account of your behavior.

If all that is true, then why do we refuse to honor God? Certainly, the problem is not that God is intrinsically dishonorable. We owe everything we have to his being. Every good gift we enjoy comes from his benevolence. But we refuse to honor God as God.

We Are Not Grateful

We heard a variety of responses when we asked students to name those to whom they attribute their achievements, successes, and the benefits that they have enjoyed. Here is their hall of honor:

> *"Yeah, if you ask me who I am grateful to first for all I have been given, I would say my family, not God. I suppose it all backtracks to God, but I think that's a little nebulous for me. You know what I mean? I need to look at something a little more substantial."*

> *"I feel grateful to God in a sense that I'm grateful for my good fortune, for the good things that have happened to me. And if I think that he has had an intervention in every one of those things, then, yes, I am grateful."*

> *"A lot of good things in my life have come from hard work. Some of it does come from my parents. Not that I was born into money, but I was very fortunate to have parents that had a little bit of money so that I could go to Tulane University, which is a very expensive school."*

"I attribute the benefits of life that I have to my own actions and to my own choices that I've made and how I have chosen to live my life."

Gratitude rises from the depths of the soul, from an honest recognition that someone else has provided that which I have received. These good things received have not been earned. To claim for myself the merit for the benefit I enjoy seems unbelievably smug. Every benefit I have ever received has come as a gift.

But is that true? Let us try a test case. Ann was born in the ghetto, and both her parents are alcoholics. She has now "earned" her graduate degree with honors. Ann paid her dues on the climb up the educational ladder—hard-won scholarship grants, flipping burgers, and waiting tables. She is certainly obliged to honor none, for she has pulled herself to the heights by her boot straps.

But is that true? While we can't build a complete biography for our scholar, we may suspect that benefactors of mercy extended a hand to Ann along the way. Here are a few of those debts:

- Ann is alive. Outside B-movie scripts, I have never heard of a corpse that achieved much success in school. Someone or something must account for the fact of her existence.
- Ann's physical needs were met by someone before she learned to meet her own needs. Not even a Rhodes scholar came into the world able to provide food, grow cotton and weave it into clothing, stake out and defend a shelter, and arrange potty training. Even if such a prodigy existed, where did the raw materials for all this self-care come from?

- Ann's mental faculties were placed within her genetic code and developed within her brain. Her mind then was nurtured by others, who also had capable brains placed within their cranial cavities. Even more fundamentally, there was a systematic universe in which knowledge exists to be learned and taught.
- Ann's emotional and social needs obviously had to be met for her to excel. There are social settings around the world in which no child has the potential to gain status and acceptance, let alone knowledge. Even with her limited background, Ann was provided with the potential for success unusual in human history. This potential includes the mercies that accumulated the wealth that scholarship benefactors gave to a scholarship fund.

I doubt there is a single college student for whom the list of mercies—human and divine—would not go on.

Have we really become so arrogant as to ignore all of these gifts? For some time I have been involved in a discipline of philosophy, theology, and discourse called *apologetics*. I think out rational issues about the existence and character of God. I talk to people and try to answer the questions they raise. I believe that there are compelling reasons to believe in the existence of God, and I believe it is good to debate them. But I go into such study and discussions with one assumption firmly in mind: a certainty that the person I am talking with already knows that God exists. The most convinced atheist is not intellectually unaware of the reality of God. The unbeliever, rather, has another problem: He or she does not like the God who is. The knowledge of God has been suppressed from the rational thought life because the person knows what is at stake.

Jonathan Edwards has been called (even in his *Encyclopedia Britannica* biographical entry) the greatest mind ever produced on the North American continent. This superlative thinker studied the human condition and declared that by nature we are hostile to God. A principal reason, Edwards said, is that God is holy, and we are not. We would rather he didn't exist; a nonexistent God is far less terrifying that One who is holy.

Questions for Study and Discussion

1. What are the differences between Paul's and Kant's perceptions of this world?
2. What is the universal reaction to the existence of a Creator Deity?
3. If creation so loudly and clearly proclaims the existence of God, why do so many people deny this truth?
4. In what ways is God being robbed of who he is? What is his reaction to this?
5. What gifts and graces has God given you throughout your life? What effect have these gifts had on your level of gratitude toward God?
6. Why are humans by nature hostile to God?

THREE

HIS WORD IS TRUTH

"I don't think the Bible is true. I think the stories were put in there to teach lessons. I study a lot of mythology. It all relates."

"We are pretty safe saying the Bible is true to some extent."

"You can't take the Bible word-for-word verbatim. You have to learn how to read it, read between the lines, and get the message out of what they were trying to say."

"I don't think you are supposed to live your life to the letter of the law of the Ten Commandments.
I think what the Ten Commandments are trying to say is to do what you think is right."

"Love God before all others. Do not use the Lord's name in vain."

"I think all the Ten Commandments, when you get down to it, are hard to live by."

As we began our previous discussion, an empty chair was pulled up to the table for Immanuel Kant. Maybe you noticed that as soon as Kant sits in, the tenor of the discussion changes. Someone suggests an answer to an ultimate issue. Each time that happens in the search for truth, old Immanuel stomps his rational foot.

> *"That is an interesting point you are making there," he says, "and you might be able to use that truth statement. It may work for you quite nicely. But of course you can't really argue that it is an ultimate answer for everyone. We can only use that word* truth *loosely. If there are real truths. I can't know what they are, and neither can you. We can only plug in our best guess and go from there.*

This is a very unsatisfying answer. If he's right, we might as well close the door and go home. Sort-a-truths don't resolve ultimate issues. I don't know about you, but I won't give in to the rationalist's defeat if I have a sane alternative. Paul gave me one.

Remember that Paul pulled another chair into the discussion circle. This is a chair for God. If there is an open universe, there is God. If God cares to sit in, Kant is wrong.

Repressed Reality

Zedekiah, for one, was desperately hoping for an open universe. He was sweating in fear when he asked his ultimate question:
Is there a word from the LORD?

Zedekiah was king of the nation of Judah, and he was asking the prophet Jeremiah his question. Don't think Zedekiah was such a lover of truth. He had not been a bit interested in hearing what Jeremiah's God had to say. In fact, he had imprisoned Jeremiah in a pit for the crime of bringing unwanted advice.

But now the most fearsome army on earth was parked on Zedekiah's doorstep. He faced a life-and-death struggle. If a word of truth was to be had, he needed it now (see Jeremiah 37).

Kant says we cannot know whether a word about God is a true word. God's existence cannot be deduced through theoretical thought, empirical investigation, or rational deduction. Paul says we need not prove God. Rational human beings know that God exists—and know it clearly. They just don't want to hear him. They suppress the evidence until it is too late, as did Zedekiah.

Remember that we quoted the Old Testament assertion:

The heavens declare the glory of God;
    the skies proclaim the work of his hands.

(PSALM 19:1)

Here the Kantian rationalist cries, "Foul!" If nature's revelation is an advertisement for God, the skeptic asks why we should believe the marketing claims:

This God that I supposedly know exists certainly looks invisible. I don't care how incredible or illogical my unbelief may seem to you Christians. I prefer to think things just happened, unless God personally tells me otherwise in words I cannot miss.

For someone who feels this way, I have bad news and good news. I already alluded to the bad news. Anyone who suppresses ultimate truth shares the futile ignorance of Zedekiah. Philosophers and ethicists—today's royal advisers—cheer from the sidelines. But when crisis comes and a real word from the Lord is needed, we will find that the God who does exist is angry.

Now the good news: The God who exists was not content to reveal himself in creation. He gives explicit, specific, and personal words that have been transmitted through speech. We can't miss them (unless we want to).

Just as in the case of creation, we *do* want to miss them. Psychologists don't speak of *suppressing* reality so much as *repressing* unconsciously what we feel uncomfortable about facing openly. Paul would probably consider that a good description of the common reaction to God's verbal revelation. The common reaction to news of a holy book from God is: "Isn't this book just the ramblings of misguided zealots?" Ironically, some psychologists provide a case study in suppression at this point. The verdict of psychological theory with a rationalistic worldview is that religion arises from a deeply rooted need for peace, meaning, or relief from guilt. Neuroses feed on religion.

Kant actually said something like this. However incorrect our senses may be, human beings, he admitted, feel a need for a god. Kant, however, could only provide them with an irrational feeling of dependence, sort-a-truth in a sort-a-god.

That approach cuts two ways. If powerful forces incline us psychologically to flee from truth, then we do not miss God because we can't see him. We miss God because it is too painful to see him and his truth. If that is so, then we had better doubt our doubts. They may not be as rational as we prefer to believe.

Repression is precisely the mental defense mechanism that Paul sees at work. He writes, "Since they did not think it worthwhile to retain the knowledge of God, he gave them over to a depraved mind" (Romans 1:28). Paul describes this as a universal human phenomenon. No human being wants God.

This, of course, doesn't stop God from existing if he does exist, or from speaking truth if he does speak it. I can repress the existence of sharks, but if sharks exist and I swim where they exist, repression won't save me. The result of trying to repress the existence of God is most unpleasant. God condemns us to sit in our own evil ignorance. We are condemned to depravity because we are determined not to let the knowledge of God penetrate our heads. We will do everything we can to escape it.

In that case, nothing should seem more suspect than our smug certainty that we see no God on the horizon. Psychology has another term for that kind of thinking. It is "delusional."

When a God Speaks

You have probably seen cars with religion-promoting bumper stickers. Some Christians like to decorate their cars with bumper-sticker messages. One popular message says, "God said it. I believe it. That settles it." This bumper sticker is bad theology. Its middle clause ignores the difference between a Creator God and those who have been created. If the Creator God says it, it is settled—whether I believe it or not. If the supremely powerful Source of ultimate truth opens his sacred mouth and utters a single word, debate is moot. The question is not whether the matter is settled once God says it.

The question is whether he has said anything. In Christianity the issue revolves around the Bible. We set the Bible apart in our thinking as *the Scriptures.* The word means "writings," but in terms of Christian faith the Scriptures are the only writings that come from the mouth of God. We commit absolutely everything to the proposition that a Creator exists, wants to be heard, and has spoken.

How radically does our religion rest on this proposition? One of the Bible's declarations is found at the beginning of the Gospel of John. This statement of our faith starts by directly equating Jesus Christ, whom we believe to be God-become-human, with *God's Word of revelation.* One thing John is saying is that an ultimate, living, human reality stands behind God's words. There is an exemplar:

> In the beginning was the Word, and the Word was with God, and the Word was God. He was with God in the beginning. Through him all things were made; without him nothing was made that has been made. In him was life, and that life was the light of men. The light shines in the darkness, but the darkness has not understood it. . . . The Word became flesh and lived for a while among us. We have seen his glory, the glory of the one and only Son, who came from the Father, full of grace and truth.
>
> (JOHN 1:1–5, 14)

Another book of the Bible, Hebrews, begins by explaining what the coming of an exemplar from God means:

> In the past God spoke to our forefathers through the prophets at many times and in various ways, but in these last days he has spoken to us by his Son, whom he appointed heir of all things, and through whom he made the universe. The Son is the radiance of God's glory and the exact representation of his being, sustaining all things by his powerful word. After he had provided purification for sins, he sat down at the right hand of the Majesty in heaven.
>
> (Hebrews 1:1–3)

Whatever you think about Christianity and the Bible, you must agree that the two are inseparable.

A camera crew took cameras and recording equipment to college campuses and asked students what they think of Scripture. Here are some of the responses:

> *"I don't think the Bible is true. I think the stories were put in there to teach lessons. I study a lot of mythology. It all relates."*
>
> *"It sounds to me like a legend that's been passed down from generation to generation. I think, as is the case with any legend, things get exaggerated, and things get distorted."*

"I think it is fascinating. I think it's beautiful. I think there is a lot of truth within it. I think there's a lot of history within it. I think there's a lot of fiction within it. I think there's a lot of culture within it."

"We are pretty safe saying the Bible is true to some extent."

"I don't think it is true for everybody, and I don't think it ever could be."

"In the context that the Bible was written in [it is true]. When you introduce science and things like that, some of it does become, let's say, dated—not necessarily untrue, but dated."

"You can't take the Bible word-for-word verbatim. You have to learn how to read it, read between the lines, and get the message out of what they were trying to say."

"I have read parts of the Bible, and I really enjoy it. I don't really have very much time to do any recreational reading aside from school work, and I don't read the Bible in my spare time."

The students used words such as *fiction, legend,* and *mythology* to describe Scripture. "There may be some truth in it, but it lies buried, as in any myth. . . . It may contain truth, but it can't possibly be true for everybody."

Logically, this cannot be an accurate assessment of the Bible. Take, for example, the central assertion of the New Testament that Jesus Christ died and was raised from the dead. If that is true in

time-and-space history for anybody, it is true for everybody. We
are not talking about parallel universes, each with individual realities. One set of historical facts is true. Read any part of the New
Testament and much of the Old Testament. Everything said there
is predicated on the fact that a Savior would later or had in the
past died and conquered death. These statements are only worthwhile if God says them, if they are so.

If they are not so—if God did not make a plan of salvation for
the human race, if Jesus did not die and rise from the dead—this
really is mythological fiction. Its only value is to be a historical
curiosity or, as one person said it, "recreational reading." If the
Bible communicates ultimate words from almighty God, it is anything but an occasion for recreation.

Here is the collision of worldviews. Not everybody agrees
about the nature of Scripture. Scripture makes claims about itself.
The personal friend and apostle of Jesus, Peter, denies that his own
testimony was a fable:

> We did not follow cleverly invented stories when we
> told you about the power and coming of our Lord Jesus
> Christ, but we were eyewitnesses of his majesty.
>
> (2 PETER 1:16)

In his advice to a young man, Paul goes further:

> Continue in what you have learned and have become
> convinced of, because you know those from whom you
> learned it, and how from infancy you have known the

holy Scriptures, which are able to make you wise for salvation through faith in Christ Jesus. All Scripture is
God-breathed.

(2 TIMOTHY 3:14–16A)

See the antithesis? Peter stood on Scripture's truthfulness, as he
himself was its witness. Peter understood the Hebrew concept of
the sanctity of truth. Deeply entrenched in his culture was a
prohibition against the bearing of false testimony. Paul adds that
Scripture contains words of truth, wisdom, and salvation, not
because they were childhood stories. Rather, they are wisdom
because they are "God-breathed."

Evaluating Truth Claims

Jesus was put on trial in the court of Pontius Pilate. Pilate
represented Roman authority, and there was no appeal from his
decisions. Not understanding why people hated Jesus so much
that they wanted to see him crucified, Pilate asked Jesus what he
was doing and whether he was trying to become the king. Jesus
answered,

For this I came into the world, to testify to the truth.
Everyone on the side of truth listens to me.

(JOHN 18:37B)

Pilate was asking Jesus to summarize the intent of his entire
mission. Jesus replied that he came to answer the question of truth.

He then made the extraordinary claim that he was the source of truth. Only those who heard him have ultimate truth in their minds.

We must see whether evidence lies behind this claim—what scholars call the *indicia*. Is there any evidential basis for the claims Scripture makes? It is outside the scope of this book to give a full-fledged apologetic for the integrity of sacred Scripture. We can sketch that apologetic path, though. This path leads from questions of general reliability to a general picture of Jesus to the question of what Jesus himself says.

A RELIABLE HISTORICAL SOURCE

A starting point for inquiry is to answer the question, Does the Bible communicate reliable, historical information? If the answer to that question is no, then there is no reason to spend even five minutes attending to its message.

I am a professional theologian. Among my academic colleagues many have concluded that Scripture is not reliable. A whole forum argues about whether a historical person named Jesus even existed. Frankly, these men and women are historiographically irresponsible. On the basis of any accepted measure of historical verification (for example, contemporary corroboration from multiple and disinterested sources, archeological and textual evidence, and evidence of identifiable impact on people or institutions), no individual in history is better attested to than Jesus of Nazareth. To dismiss all that demonstrates unworthy research bias.

Scripture's testimony is at least as reliable as the work of the ancient historians Tacitus or Heroditus. Abraham Herschel, a modern Judaic theologian and archeologist, singled out the writer of the Gospel of Luke and the Acts for special note. Luke, said Herschel, is the most trustworthy historian of antiquity. For such a knowledgeable non-Christian to make that statement is significant.

A SUFFICIENT HISTORICAL SOURCE

Let's assume that this information is at the very least generally reliable. Can we glean enough information from this historical document to give us a picture of the historical Jesus? There seems little reason for skepticism on that point. Probably the greatest archeologist who ever lived, William Foxwell Albright, contributed to the Anchor Bible series, one of the most prestigious critical analyses of the Bible. In the introduction he wrote for that series he expressed frustration at the intrusion of existential categories of philosophy into biblical scholarship. This agenda destroys the scientific nature of biblical studies, Albright said. Albright, whose own rigorous objectivity is legendary, called this pseudoscholarship a negative influence that warps and distorts efforts to evaluate the historical content of the New Testament.

If we accept the Gospel of Luke as accurate history, we might as well accept the Gospels of Matthew and Mark, since they agree with Luke so closely that most New Testament scholars believe all three Gospel writers had access to the same source document. John's Gospel takes a more philosophical and personal approach, but objective Bible students admit that his facts tally with the other three. Acts is a continuation of the Gospel of Luke that tells the story of the founding and earliest outreach of Christian faith after

Jesus returned to heaven. Other books of the New Testament can be fit into the time line set by the Book of Acts.

Now, if we know anything about Jesus of Nazareth, it is safe to conclude that he was at least an authentic prophet. That is the judgment of the Christian church, many Jews, Muslims, and even non-Christians of other varieties. "I will give you this much," I have heard people say, "I don't believe Jesus is God incarnate, and I don't believe he was raised from the dead, but he was a man committed to the truth."

THE CLAIM OF JESUS

These points lead to yet another question: What did Jesus himself teach about the Scriptures? In higher critical theories, where skepticism reigns, a majority of scholars say some of the documents in the New Testament were written by later editors. These editors supposedly mixed early information and fragments with later documents, usually to advance their own agenda. So now we must try to distinguish the core information about which there is no question.

A striking thing about this radical "redaction criticism" is that the critics have never found legitimate reason to challenge most of Jesus' own comments about the integrity of Scripture. Passages in which Jesus declares that the Scriptures are the Word of God are seldom tagged as inauthentic. Even most skeptics believe that the historical person of Jesus of Nazareth made such statements as the following:

In them is fulfilled the prophecy of Isaiah. . . .

(MATTHEW 13:14A)

You are in error because you do not know the Scriptures or the power of God.

(MATTHEW 22:29)

But this has all taken place that the writings of the prophets might be fulfilled.

(MATTHEW 26:56)

The Scriptures must be fulfilled.

(MARK 14:49)

Everything must be fulfilled that is written about me in the Law of Moses, the Prophets, and the Psalms.

(LUKE 24:44B)

The Scripture cannot be broken.

(JOHN 10:35B)

You diligently study the Scriptures because you think that by them you possess eternal life. These are the Scriptures that testify about me, yet you refuse to come to me to have life.

(JOHN 5:39–40)

THE INTEGRITY OF JESUS' CLAIM

Scholars do say, "Yes, Jesus taught that the Bible was the veritable word of God inspired, infallible, and all of that, but of course Jesus was only a human being, and he was simply wrong." This would make Jesus a false prophet, because as the above verses and a number of others show, Jesus claimed infallible knowledge and authority to make such claims. He would be teaching falsehood about a question of ultimate importance.

The Price of Ignorance

Listening to those comments about the Bible from students, I was reminded that it is not enough to establish the nature of Scripture. These students don't know enough Scripture content to make an informed decision. No wonder they haven't come to grips with it. Nor are they alone. In a survey in Denver, Colorado, professing Christians were asked to name at least five of the Ten Commandments. Few could do it. If any of them have the bumper sticker, "God said it. I believe it. That settles it," they live most unsettled lives.

When we asked students about the commandments of God and whether they take them seriously, we got interesting responses:

"He knew what he was doing. I mean if you take the Ten Commandments and if you follow them, then things in the world are just going to go together. If people don't steal, if they don't lie or cheat, then you know it's obvious that people are just going to get along."

"Love God before all other. Do not use the Lord's name in vain."

"Well, I believe that the Ten Commandments should be followed, but sometimes a time comes when you must disobey one."

"Do not make any idols. Do not kill."

"The Ten Commandments, or whatever, they make sense. You should treat other people the way you want to be treated."

"Umm. Do not covet what is others'."

"I don't know all of them, but I am sure I have broken at least one of them in my life."

"Do not commit adultery."

"I think all the Ten Commandments, when you get down to it, are hard to live by."

"No. Not one commandment is hard to obey."

"I don't think you are supposed to live your life to the letter of the law of the Ten Commandments. I think what

*the Ten Commandments are trying to say is to do what you
think is right."*

*"I guess if I lived in Salem they would have me in the
water right now."*

The girl who worried about being dunked with the witches in
Salem had actually done a better job of naming the commandments
than most people. But the point is not how many of the ten we can
name. More important is whether we hear what they are saying.

The student who admitted he might have broken one commandment during his lifetime reminds me of a man who came up
to Jesus (Matthew 19:16–22) and asked, "Teacher, what good thing
must I do to get eternal life?"

"Why do you ask me about what is good?" Jesus replied.
"There is only One who is good. If you want to enter life, obey
the commandments."

"Which ones?"

" 'Do not murder, do not commit adultery, do not steal, do
not give false testimony, honor your father and mother,' and 'love
your neighbor as yourself.' "

"All these I have kept," the young man said. "What do I still lack?"

This man could probably have listed all Ten Commandments,
but he hadn't been listening. He did know that something was miss-
ing. Jesus knew his problem, so he challenged the man's assumptions.

"Wait a minute," Jesus said. "Why are you calling me good?
Nobody is good but God." Jesus wasn't denying that he was God
or that he was good. He knew the fellow was just spouting a casual

view of goodness to impress him. Since the man was talking about "good" things, Jesus said, "Okay, you know the commandments."

"Oh, is that all?" responded the man. "I've done all that."

Then Jesus cut that confidence out from under him: "Oh, that's wonderful. Just one little thing. Go and sell all you have, give it to the poor, and follow me."

The man's mouth dropped at that. Matthew 19:22 records that he walked away sad, because he had great possessions.

To the man's credit, he didn't argue, "What are you pulling? The commandments don't say anything about giving your money away." Maybe he was starting to hear the first commandment when God thundered: "You shall have no other gods before me." He didn't know he had made a god of possessions until Jesus gave him a pop quiz: "Let's start with commandment number one. Go sell everything you have. Find out if you have other gods."

If we don't struggle with the Word of God, it is only because we are so ignorant of it. Ignorance of Scripture is pervasive in our culture. Why? The primary reason is that the subject is ignored. We ignore the Bible. We don't want to think about God. We want to banish him from intruding, particularly when he makes a claim on our lives and impulses. In my natural self it is easier if there are no ultimate realities in a revealed word from God. I prefer that such a revelation be a myth because I want to be free of its obligation. I have a conflict over the ultimate issue of authority. If I exercise personal autonomy, I am a law unto myself. I can do anything I want because I want.

If that is where we are, we had better hope that there is no God and no law or that God is dumb and deaf and blind.

But don't bet your life on it.

QUESTIONS FOR STUDY AND DISCUSSION

1. Other than creation, what means has God used to reveal himself?

2. Why is the rejection of the truth of God's Word a natural human reaction?

3. Why is it illogical to believe that the Bible can be true for one person and not true for another?

4. What evidence exists to support the reliability and integrity of Scripture?

5. Do you believe that God's Word is truth? Why or why not?

6. What is at the heart of the Ten Commandments? What are they saying?

F O U R

CHRIST, THE ONLY WAY

"I'd have to say, 'Because
I always did what I felt
was right, and I always
followed my own beliefs.'"

"I've probably disobeyed
many, many commandments,
but I don't really think that
that should influence my
behavior as a good person."

"The gospel is fundamental
belief that God sent his
Son to earth to live out
a human life—a perfect
human life."

"I think, number one, I'd have a lot of explaining to do about some parts of my life, some of my philosophies."

"I believe he came to take away the sins of the world, and I believe he was crucified on the cross. I believe he is coming back."

"But there are people out there that are worse than me. I mean, that might be the basis of my belief. There is always someone worse. He can't keep everyone out. If there is a heaven, you know—he will let me in."

CONVERSATION AROUND THE COFFEEHOUSE table should stimulate creative thinking and understanding. Unfortunately, sometimes it generates pooled idiocy. You probably have experienced the latter sort of discussion. Camaraderie may be warm. Everyone has a view to throw out onto the floor—until you are all ankle-deep in hogwash. No one has done the thinking needed to formulate a meaningful opinion, let alone sustain it by logical arguments. That is no way to approach ultimate issues.

Sure answers to the ultimate questions of life *are* available. You can get them from their Source. Certain proof for ultimate truth exists only if a rational Creator God has purposefully revealed truths about himself. I believe

- that precisely such revelation has occurred.
- that I see the broad outline of that revelation in the warp and woof of the universe.
- that these answers can be readily perceived in the Bible.
- that the Bible is "holy" Scriptures because God directly interacted in the lives, experiences, and thoughts of the authors.
- that God stakes his divine integrity on his claim that the Bible answers ultimate questions without error.

This does not limit me to the Bible in my attempt to find answers to questions. There is much to learn from the accumulated wisdom of human history. But the Bible is the only certain map by which to chart travel toward answers to *ultimate* questions. The Bible serves as a fixed reference point from which to distinguish truth among the sayings of the wise. It is the instruction manual for life. With its schematics I can build a philosophy that takes into account the universe as it truly is, God as he truly is, and myself as I truly am.

I am elated by that news, until I read what the revelation contained in the Bible says.

It tells me that life is messed up.

It tells me that God is angry at the reasons life is messed up.

It tells me that I am one of the reasons life is messed up.

In bold letters the Manufacturer's advisory reads,

WARNING

SMALL IS THE GATE AND NARROW IS THE ROAD

THAT LEADS TO LIFE,

AND ONLY A FEW FIND IT

Imagine reading this sign and suddenly realizing you are standing on a tiny piece of firm ground in the center of a quicksand bog. There's one narrow path out, and it can be seen only by aligning your line of sight on a distant gate. Any deviation from this unseen path leads to disaster. Would you be motivated to hold your sights on the gates, accepting no substitutes? The above warning, from Matthew 7:14, is part of an authoritative *forensic declaration*.

Forensic Testimony

High school and college students can take part in forensic classes or forensic competitions. The general public became well acquainted with the term *forensic* during the twentieth century's most publicized criminal trial. O. J. Simpson's freedom hung on the jury's take on the forensic statements made from the witness stand and forensic evidence collected by police. The jury had to decide whether this evidence convincingly proved that the accused had killed Nicole Brown Simpson and Ronald Goldman.

Forensics has to do with declarations of truth that come during a formal proceeding. We usually think of them in relation to legal matters or in debates and public speaking. Somebody stands and "declares." The prosecution argues that physical evidence "declares." Criminologists, the coroner, and other "forensic experts" present evidence and "declare." Finally the opposing attorneys give their closing arguments, which try to interpret the forensic evidence as proof that they stand in the right.

Only after the forensic evidence is laid out can a verdict properly be reached by a jury, a judgment made, and a pronouncement uttered.

One of history's most crucial trials in which forensic testimony was presented came during an April week in 1521. The atmosphere must have been intense throughout the German city of Worms when a watchman in the tower of the city cathedral blew his horn to announce the arrival of a great celebrity. A great many people gawked and cheered.

The center of attention was an unassuming man in a monk's cowl, a university professor named Martin Luther who rode into town in a small covered wagon pulled by three horses.

Luther had been advised that if he went to Worms to stand trial for his views he might well be arrested and burned at the stake. He would go anyway, he said, though "demons be as many as tiles on the house roofs." He came voluntarily, to defend himself of a charge of heresy before Emperor Charles V of the Holy Roman

Empire and the German nobility, plus Oleander the papal nuncio and cardinals of the church.

It is easy to see how forensic evidence applies in a murder trial. But how does it apply to a man like Martin Luther, or to us? The answer to that question is what the rest of this book will consider. The central issue of the sixteenth-century debate was the question, "How can an unjust person be *forensically justified* in the presence of God?" We can also phrase this question in these terms: "Where is the declarative evidence that will save me from a guilty verdict and a sentence of eternal condemnation?" "How does the work of Christ and his ministry relate to me, centuries after Jesus lived?" "Is there a *gospel* (meaning 'good news')? If so, what is its hopeful message?"

These questions get to the core of the most ultimate issue of all.

Why Jesus Came

On college campuses we asked students, "What do you understand to be the reason or the purpose for Jesus coming to this earth?"

"I think Jesus' main goal was to forgive sins of the world when he died on the cross, crucifixion. I think that was his main purpose when he came here."

"I think it is so hard to try to comprehend this today why somebody had to come and die. We don't have to make the sacrifices anymore. Back in the old days when they had to take the different animals and sacrifice them and that was how they did it, then the ultimate sacrifice was Jesus

coming down. I think that is kind of one reason that it is so hard to understand why someone had to die."

"I think he came to try and get people to be a little nicer to each other, if anything, and obviously it didn't work."

"I believe he came to take away the sins of the world, and I believe he was crucified on the cross. I believe he is coming back."

"The gospel is fundamental belief that God sent his Son to earth to live out a human life—a perfect human life."

"When you have the ability to persuade thousands and thousands of people, it goes to your head. Maybe he could do great things, I'm not going to doubt that. I didn't live back then, and I really haven't read that much Scripture, but if you claim to be God and I feel you are a man, well . . . But I'm getting in trouble here."

At least the latter student had a sense that there was a possibility of getting in trouble here. I think we all understand that the worst possible trouble we could ever encounter would be to come before a court in a trial of ultimate judgment. It's one thing to be sitting in a cell in Los Angeles on trial for your life, as was O. J. Simpson. It's quite another thing to stand before the imperial Diet of Worms where Luther stood in the sixteenth century. And it is quite another altogether to stand before your Creator.

In this latter trial you are summoned not for one thing you did, but for the worth of your entire life. And to stand before a

God who is utterly and absolutely holy and in his holiness, perfectly just. Imagine being summoned into that environment, to be called into the courtroom of God, to be judged by the standard of his perfection.

A few years ago I spoke at a national conference of Christian booksellers. About six thousand people were there, all involved in the business of producing or selling religious literature. At first, I didn't know what to speak about. I finally decided on the question, "What does it mean to be saved?"

I was a bit intimidated. If I went to that convention to speak on such an elementary subject, surely I would insult the audience's intelligence. These men and women have access to the greatest compilation of religious writing in history. Surely they know what it means to be saved. I began with the apology that I didn't want to offend them by asking the most rudimentary question of all: "Are you saved?"

Sometimes, especially around college campuses, overbearing zealots will go up to people, figuratively grab them by the throat, and ask:

"Are you saved?" When that happens to me, I want to say, "Saved from what? I am certainly not saved from people who impolitely intrude on my tranquility."

"That's the question I am here to ask," I told the bookstore people. " 'Saved from what?' What the New Testament says is that we were saved from God."

My audience looked baffled. I could read their thoughts perfectly: "No, no, no, no, Professor Sproul. It's not that we're saved *from* God; we are saved *by* God. God is our salvation. God has sent Jesus into the world to be our Savior so it is God who is doing the saving. He is saving us from our sins."

Yes, it is true that God sent Jesus into the world. And yes, Jesus does save us from our sins. But do you ever think about *why Jesus needs to save us from our sins?* How can our sins hurt us? Once they are gone, they are over with.

I love to play golf, but I hate it when the ball slices to the side. Then I have to hit a difficult shot to get from where I am to where I want to be. It's an ugly situation. But once it is over it is over. I breathe a sigh of relief and say, "Glad I don't ever have to hit that shot again. It's history."

Why shouldn't it be that way with sins? They make life awfully messy. But usually it takes a relatively brief bit of pain to get through the consequences of stupidity. Then it's history, isn't it? Unfortunately, no, because I don't have to worry about being saved from my past sins. I have to worry about a holy God who remains angry about my past sins. I need to be saved *from* God.

God's anger is the *ultimate* ultimate issue.

A couple of the students recognized that what Jesus Christ did had something to do with the sacrifices of the Old Testament. But it all seems rather vague why Jesus Christ's death is connected on one end to the Old Testament sacrifices and on the other end to my personal life. Given what we have said about God's justice, obviously the Old Testament sacrifices did not cancel sin. Sin is rebellion against an infinite God and requires an infinite penalty to satisfy an infinite demand for justice.

No, the point of the sacrifice was to give forensic testimony. This testimony reminded the sinner of personal need before God. It was forensic testimony that declared: "I am guilty. This is a debt I cannot pay. If there is to be mercy, then someone else must pay for my crime."

And the sacrifice declared that one day the necessary sacrifice—the real payment to satisfy divine justice—would be made.

For the forensic testimony to be adequate evidence in this trial, the punishment would have to be as infinite as the crime. The punished would have to be as innocent as this helpless animal whose throat was cut—and would have to be an infinite being.

Only God himself could present the required forensic testimony.

At Collision Ground-Zero

It would be terrifying to be on a planet in the vicinity of the impact point of a comet. Comet ground-zero is not the most frightening place to be, however. The most frightening place is the point at which my sin collides with God's justice, justice that demands absolute perfection. Against the standard of God, I am not just. Are you? If I have to stand in God's courtroom, all the forensic evidence screams that I am guilty.

We now return to Martin Luther at his trial before the emperor. Luther was charged with teaching error. What bothered the church was that he taught that the New Testament answer to humanity's ultimate issue is what might be called *forensic justification.* It was at the point of forensic justification that Luther made his ringing response to the demand that he recant his beliefs:

"Here I stand. I can do no other. God help me, amen."

God grant that each of us makes this stand non-negotiable. Forensic justification is nothing less than that justification that comes when God himself declares that you stand before him as if you have never sinned.

The only way you can ever be justified is if God says you are justified. You can give him no such forensic testimony as,

"Hey, I never sinned."

"I tried to live a good life."

"Yes, I did some wrong, but my heart was in the right place . . . somewhat . . . mostly."

What you need is for God to give a verdict that says, "You are just in my sight."

How can God declare people just when they're not? That would be a lie. The Roman Catholic Church reacted strongly to Luther's doctrine of "justification by faith alone" because it was convinced that it involved a legal fiction. Luther said that the sinner who is justified by Christ is *simul justus et peccator*. We can break down this Latin phrase to understand what he meant:

Simul, "simultaneously, at the same time"
Justus, "just"
Et, "and" (No, it's not the past tense of *eat.)*
Peccator, "sinner"
Simul justus et peccator—"At the same time just and sinner"

How can that be? Luther said this phrase communicates the essence of the gospel. At the very moment in which we are guilty, God freely and graciously pronounces us to be just. That is his verdict when, in reality, we aren't just. Doesn't this cast a shadow over the integrity of God? Is God allowing blind justice to peak over the blindfold? Is God saying, "I am going to call you just, though we both know you are not?"

That's not the way it works. God does have the right to consider you to be just, for in fact the infinite penalty for the sins with which we are charged has been paid. God paid them himself. Your sin was *imputed* to Jesus Christ; his righteousness was *imputed* to you.

The Naked Truth

Imputation means a kind of "transfer." We seldom encounter this precise concept in life. To "impute" something is to transfer it legally to someone else's account.

In the drama of religious worship in Old Testament Israel, the holiest day of the year was the Day of Atonement, *Yom Kippur.* On Yom Kippur the high priest would offer special sacrifices that happened only on this day once a year. At one point in this solemn ceremony, the priest placed his hands on the head of a goat. In so doing, he symbolically laid the sins of the people on this innocent animal. The English translation of what they called that goat remains in our culture. It was the "scapegoat." After placing the sins of the people on the goat, it was driven out from the camp into the wilderness to perish. The goat died outside the camp, for it was accounted guilty in the place of the people.

Imputation works in two ways. Remember that some of the students, when asked what Jesus did, said that he came to earth to die. They said the purpose for Jesus coming to this world was to die on the cross. Actually, that's a half truth. If that were the only purpose for Christ coming to this world, he could have come down as a grown man on a parachute, gone straight to Jerusalem, died on the cross, and it would have been finished. But he didn't just come to die. Somebody else said Jesus came to live a perfect life. That is another pie of the puzzle: He came both to live, and then to die. He came to live under the law of God. He said, "It is necessary that I fulfill the law" (see, for example, Matthew 3:15). So the most astonishing thing about the life of Jesus is not that he was raised from the dead, but that he lived in complete righteousness through a life of perfect obedience. You and I cannot think and do perfect obedience before God for five minutes.

On that basis there is a twofold imputation. On the one hand, God transferred the guilt of his people to Christ on the cross. He counted Jesus worthy of hell. He reckoned Jesus worthy of his wrath. The Father forsook him in that punishment on the cross because he had willingly received this forensic, legal transfer of guilt from my account to his account. In so doing, he paid the penalty that I deserved.

But all that imputation does is get me back to square one. That makes me innocent in the sight of God, but it doesn't make me righteous in his sight. For me to pass the bar of God's ultimate tribunal, I must possess real righteousness. Where do I get it? At the heart of the gospel, the point at which Luther said we stand or fall, is the idea that I am redeemed through the death of Christ. I am righteous through the life of Christ. I can stand before God because I am accounted the righteousness Jesus merited as perfect God become perfect human on my behalf. The righteousness that God desires is imputed forensically to every human being who puts faith in him.

What are the grounds by which you can be just, though a sinner, before God? Luther said it this way: The righteousness by which we are justified is a righteousness that is apart from us. It is outside of us. It is not our own righteousness, although it becomes our own once God declares it to be ours.

In his sight, it is ours.

The Bible uses the imagery of nakedness. In the garden the first human beings committed the first sin of rebellion against God. Immediately they felt shame. They became aware that they were naked—uncovered before watching eyes, indecently exposed. That feeling of exposure has provided the theme for a lot of uncomfortable midnight dreams. From Freud on, psychology has tried to deal with our common feelings of indecency and shame. This is the root for that psychological disease. The first action after the first sin was to run and hide. And God began the work of redemption after the fall by dealing with that shame as soon as he came upon his mentally and physically unclothed children.

Unlike some modern psychological theorists, God began the process by confronting the offenders with the real reason for their shame. They were not guilty because they were physically unclothed. They were ashamed because they had dirtied themselves before the Creator. Next he made quite clear the consequences of that sin. They were real and significant consequences. But they were not only for the sake of God's holiness. Genesis tells us that God drove out Adam and Eve from their home because in that garden God had intended that they live on and on with him forever. Had they lived forever in their guilt and shame, Eden would have become a hell of separation from God. Physical death is part of the consequence for sin, but it also is part of God's mercy to sinners.

But once he had judged the man and the woman, God in some way reached into the hiding place of Adam and Eve to tenderly, mercifully, and graciously clothe his naked creatures.

That image extends throughout Scripture. If we were to stand naked before God on the strength of our own virtue (or our lack of it), we would certainly perish before the gaze of his purity. But Christ came to produce a righteousness. Theologians call it *iustitium alienum*— "alien righteousness." This is an alien, a foreign, an extraterrestrial righteousness that God transfers to our account legally. Luther called this the article upon which the church stands or falls, because those whose nakedness has been covered in Christ are the church.

The Ultimate Issue

Since this is so, I am terrified by contemporary ideas of what it takes to satisfy the demands of a holy God. We asked the students a final question: "If you were to die tonight, and you stood before God, and if God said to you, 'Why should I let you into my heaven?' What would you say to God?"

> *"If I died tonight and God asked me why he should let me into his kingdom . . . umm . . . I would say . . . I would just kind of look at him and, you know, probably tremble."*

> *"Like, well, you looked over me all my seventeen years, and I've been nothing but good, so I have every right to be in there."*

"I've probably disobeyed many, many commandments, but I don't really think that that should influence my behavior as a good person."

"If you want to try to plead on anything, you're not going to say the whole story. I would sit there and most likely say the good things I have done. There are many bad things I've done. I know I'm not going to bring them up, but God knows them."

"I think, number one, I'd have a lot of explaining to do about some parts of my life, some of my philosophies."

"But there are people out there that are worse than me. I mean that might be the basis of my belief. There is always someone worse. He can't keep everyone out. If there is a heaven, you know—he will let me in."

"I don't think I would try to give an answer. Umm. I think, boy, I would feel that I was either coming or going at that point, and. . . ."

"I'd have to say, 'Because I always did what I felt was right, and I always followed my own beliefs.' "

"Just from everything that people have told me, there is supposed to be a just God, and, I don't know, I guess I don't really answer it."

I think those responses mirror the great cross-section of ways people think they will survive the judgment of God. Almost every single person we asked was relying on his or her own goodness. This convinces me that most people are unaware of one of two things. Many aren't aware of either of them.

First, they don't know who God is.

Second, they don't know who they are.

God is perfect and we are not. And our righteousness is not righteousness enough. The Old Testament prophet Isaiah said (Isaiah 64:6) all of our own righteousness is like filthy rags when we place them before the standard of authentic righteousness. That's why the only way a human being can possibly stand before God is that he must be clothed with true righteousness. The only supply source I know for that is Jesus Christ.

When Martin Luther said that justification is by faith alone, he meant that justification is trusting in the righteousness of Christ—in the righteousness of Christ alone. This is the message of grace. This is the provision that God has made for you. He has made no other. If you confess your sins and bow yourself in submission, and rely on Christ's righteousness instead of your own, then God promises you the total cleansing of yourself in his sight, the right to become a child of God (John 1:12–13).

That's the gospel.

What you do with it is the ultimate issue.

Questions for Study and Discussion

1. What does the Bible reveal about the state of the universe, who God is, and who you are?
2. From what does humanity need to be saved? Why?

3. Why did Jesus come to this world?

4. How is it possible to be a sinner and yet be perfectly blameless before God at the same time?

5. What is the only proper response to the question, "Why should I let you into heaven?"

6. How would you respond to someone who asked you, "How can I become a child of God?"

R. C. SPROUL (Drs. Free University of Amsterdam) is the founder and president of Ligonier Ministries, and he serves as senior minister of preaching and teaching at St. Andrews Chapel, Lake Mary, Florida. He is host of the national daily radio program *Renewing Your Mind,* and he speaks at many conferences. Sproul has written more than sixty books, including *The Holiness of God, Faith Alone, Chosen by God, Grace Unknown, The Glory of Christ, The Mystery of the Holy Spirit,* and *Getting the Gospel Right.* He is also editor of *Reformation Study Bible.*